THIS BOOK BELONGS TO

Written by James Clements

PUFFIN BOOKS

UK | USA | Canada | Ireland | Australia
India | New Zealand | South Africa

Puffin Books is part of the Penguin Random House group of companies whose addresses can be found at global.penguinrandomhouse.com.
www.penguin.co.uk   www.puffin.co.uk   www.ladybird.co.uk

Roald Dahl quotations from *The BFG* (1982, 2022), *The Witches* (1983, 2022), *Billy and the Minpins* (1991, 2022), *James and the Giant Peach* (1961, 2022), *The Giraffe and the Pelly and Me* (1985, 2022), *The Magic Finger* (1966, 2022), *Fantastic Mr Fox* (1970, 2022), *Matilda* (1988, 2023), *Charlie and the Great Glass Elevator* (1972, 2022), *Danny the Champion of the World* (1975, 2023), *Charlie and the Chocolate Factory* (1964, 2022), *George's Marvellous Medicine* (1981, 2022) and *The Twits* (1980, 2022). All titles are published by Puffin Books.
First published 2026
001

Text copyright © The Roald Dahl Story Company Ltd, 2026
Illustrations copyright © Quentin Blake, 2026
ROALD DAHL is a registered trademark of The Roald Dahl Story Company Ltd.

www.roalddahl.com

The moral right of Roald Dahl and Quentin Blake has been asserted

Penguin Random House values and supports copyright. Copyright fuels creativity, encourages diverse voices, promotes freedom of expression and supports a vibrant culture. Thank you for purchasing an authorized edition of this book and for respecting intellectual property laws by not reproducing, scanning or distributing any part of it by any means without permission. You are supporting authors and enabling Penguin Random House to continue to publish books for everyone. No part of this book may be used or reproduced in any manner for the purpose of training artificial intelligence technologies or systems. In accordance with Article 4(3) of the DSM Directive 2019/790, Penguin Random House expressly reserves this work from the text and data mining exception.

Printed in China

The authorized representative in the EEA is Penguin Random House Ireland,
Morrison Chambers, 32 Nassau Street, Dublin D02 YH68

A CIP catalogue record for this book is available from the British Library

ISBN: 978-0-241-61118-0

All correspondence to:
Puffin Books
Penguin Random House Children's
One Embassy Gardens, 8 Viaduct Gardens, London SW11 7BW

Remarkable Words
for Reading

WELCOME, REMARKABLE READERS!

Words are wonderful things. They can tell the most amazing stories and share fascinating information.

If you can unlock the meaning of the words you meet, you can be transported to magnificent chocolate factories, journey across Giant Country, or talk with fantastic foxes.

In this book, you'll be introduced to lots of *splendiferous* words, big and small, and discover how to become a word detective, puzzling out the meaning of new words you find.

Roald Dahl's stories contain some of the most wondrous and exciting descriptions of places, people and things you can find. As you make your way through this book, you'll find lots of snippets from your favourite Roald Dahl tales, showing how the magic of words can work.

So jump in and become a reading champion!

HOW TO USE THIS BOOK

You don't have to read the pages of this book in order – you can jump to the sections you find most interesting, but together the chapters of this book will help you to become a remarkable reader!

The activities on each page will help you to expand your vocabulary and unlock the meaning of any book you choose to read, with clever reading strategies and important words. Remember, if you need some extra help understanding new words, you can always look them up in a dictionary.

In the final chapter (pages 82–91), you can put your skills into practice and show off your new vocabulary superpowers by answering some questions based on Roald Dahl's books.

Are you ready? Let's read!

CONTENTS

Word detectives — 8
Using context — 10
Rooting out words — 12
Prefixes and suffixes — 14

Living things — 16
People — 18
Animals and birds — 20
Plants and trees — 22
Magical creatures — 24
Feelings and emotions — 26
Movements and actions — 28
Speaking and voices — 30
The senses — 32

Places and settings — 34
At home — 36
Cities and towns — 38
Countryside and nature — 40
Wild places — 42
Seas and oceans — 44
Beyond the Earth — 46
Extraordinary places — 48

Objects and items 50
Food 52
Transport 54
Inventors and inventions 56
Potions and spells 58

Little words, big difference 60
Determiners 62
Modal verbs 64
Conjunctions 66
Understanding phrases 68

Making sense of words 70
Making predictions 72
Making inferences 74
Visualize it 76
Skimming and scanning 78
Clarifying and summarizing 80

Putting it into practice 82
Danny's challenge 84
James's challenge 86
The BFG's challenge 88
Matilda's challenge 90

My splendiferous dictionary 92

WORD DETECTIVES

Words are the key to reading well. The stronger our vocabulary, the easier it is to make sense of books and other content.

Your vocabulary is growing all the time – you discover new words in books, conversations, school, TV programmes and games. What new words have you come across recently? Write down as many as you can think of below.

Sometimes you will meet an unfamiliar word. Don't panic! This section is about what you can do when you come across a word you're not sure about and you need to work out the meaning.

By the end of the section, you'll be ready for anything!

Offering some advice

Matilda teaches herself to read and meets a lot of new words. Sometimes she sees a new word that she doesn't know the meaning of yet. What would you do if you were her? Write some things Matilda could try below. You can always come back and add in more ideas later.

USING CONTEXT

One way to work out an unfamiliar or invented word's meaning is to use context – how it relates to the words and sentences around it – to figure out what it means.

Can you work out what *plexicated* means in this passage from *The BFG*? Write your answer in the box below.

"Stay there please," he said, "and no chittering. I is needing to listen only to silence when I is mixing up such a knotty plexicated dream as this."

Plexicated describes a 'knotty' dream, and the BFG needs silence to make one. Knotty means difficult and people often need silence to concentrate, so we can guess that *plexicated* probably means complicated.

Can you use *plexicated* in a sentence?

_____
_____
_____
_____

Use context to work out what the words in bold mean in the sentences from some Roald Dahl stories below. Underline the answer you think is the best match.

"I'm getting a bit old to go bird's nesting. Those ruddy **gruntles** always nest very high up."

A bird
A loud noise
A tall tree

"You're in a bit of a **twizzler**, aren't you?" the voice was saying. "You can't go down again because if you do you'll be guzzled up at once."

A sweet
A tricky situation
A windmill

"Hold your breaths!" the BFG whispered down to her. "Cross your **figglers**! Here we go!"

A fruit bun
Small pieces of wood
Fingers

In *James and the Giant Peach*, the Centipede sings about his favourite foods:

"I often eat boiled slobbages. They're grand when served beside
Minced doodlebugs and curried slugs. And have you ever tried
Mosquitoes' toes and wampfish roes
Most delicately fried?"

Which words and phrases are unfamiliar to you? Use context to work out what they might mean.

Unfamiliar words and phrases	What I think they mean

ROOTING OUT WORDS

Another way to work out unfamiliar words is to see if any part of the word is related to another word that you know already. These small building blocks of words are called "root words".

Look at the box below with the root word TELE in it. Then look at the other boxes and fill in the gaps. You can use a dictionary to help!

TELE	PORT	SPEC
television telephone televise teleport telescope	porter transport import export portable deport	inspect spectrum spectator spectacle
Telescope: allows you to see far into the distance

Telephone: lets you speak to someone far away | If something is portable, you can _____ | Inspect: _____ |
| **"tele" means "far"** | **"port" means "carry"** | **"spec" means "look" or "see"** |

THERM	GRAPH	MIN
thermometer thermal thermostat hypothermia	graph graphic autograph	minor minuscule
Thermometer: _____	Autograph: _____	Minuscule: _____
"therm" means "heat"	**"graph" means "write"**	**"min" means "small"**

Read the descriptions of scenes from *James and the Giant Peach*. Use what you learnt on page 12 to answer the questions.

The giant peach charged across the road, knocking over a telegraph pole and flattening two parked cars as it went by.

Which word means a post with wires that carry messages a long way? _____

The peach grew larger and larger. In half a minute, it was the size of a melon!

Which word means a small unit of time? _____

Aunt Spiker wore steel-rimmed spectacles that fixed on to the end of her nose with a clip.

Which word is another word for glasses? _____

Helicopters landed all over the hill, and out of them poured newspaper and television reporters.

Which word means someone who shares news with people? _____

Beyond the book

If you get stuck on a word, you can see if it is in the same word family as any other words you know. You could keep a list of useful root words to help you remember!

PREFIXES AND SUFFIXES

Prefixes come at the start of a word, like **un**happy or **un**kind. Suffixes come at the end of a word, as in The Ladder**less** Window-Cleaning Company from *The Giraffe and the Pelly and Me*.

Adding prefixes or suffixes to a word can change its meaning.

We can use prefixes to give a word the opposite meaning. Choose the correct prefix for each word and write it below to give the word its opposite meaning.

dis-	un-	im-	in-	il-	non-

_____ happy _____ agree _____ stop _____ logical

_____ appear _____ visible _____ legal _____ fiction

_____ possible _____ do _____ sense _____ usual

Read the sentence below, then use your knowledge of prefixes to answer the questions.

"I don't like to sound ungrateful or pushy," murmured the Giraffe, "but we do have one very pressing problem. We are all absolutely famished. We haven't eaten for days."

"My dear *Giraffey*!" cried the Duke. "How very thoughtless of me. Food is no problem around here."

Was Giraffe worrying about being thankful? _____

Which word tells you? _____

Was the Duke being considerate to his guests? _____

Which word tells you? _____

Match the suffixes to their meanings. Use the example words to help you.

-less
meaningless   clueless   harmless

-ness
laziness   goodness   happiness

-est
largest   smallest   happiest

-ful
beautiful   joyful   peaceful

-ify
magnify   stupefy   horrify

being in a state of

being full of or having lots of a quality

to make or become something

without or having none

the superlative – the highest degree or amount

Think of all the words you know that use prefixes and suffixes and write them below. Which prefix or suffix have you used most?

LIVING THINGS

People write about all manner of living creatures: real, imaginary and those that do exist but seem unbelievable!

In this section, you'll meet some words that really bring weird and wonderful creatures to life.

Before you get started, write down some of your favourite words for each category.

People

tall, folk

Birds and animals

reptile, furry

Magical creatures

unicorn, fire-breathing

Feelings and emotions

cheerful, grumpily

Movements and actions

sleepily, take a stroll

Voices and speaking

booming, whisper

PEOPLE

There are many wonderful words to describe people. Reading about a character's personality, appearance and age helps you to imagine them when you meet them in a book.

People come in all <u>ages</u>, from <u>newborn</u> to <u>elderly</u>. <u>Young</u> people might be <u>youthful</u> or <u>immature</u>. Older people might be <u>mature</u> or <u>senior</u>. However old you are, you can still be <u>childish</u>!

People have bodies or physiques of all <u>shapes and sizes</u>. Small people might be <u>short</u> or <u>knee-high to a grasshopper</u>. Tall ones might be <u>lofty</u> or <u>immense</u>. Bodies might be <u>slender</u> and <u>wiry</u>, <u>plump</u> or <u>muscular</u>.

People might be <u>kind</u>, <u>good-hearted</u>, <u>honourable</u> or <u>virtuous</u>. Or they might be <u>mean</u>, <u>cruel</u>, <u>spiteful</u>, <u>malevolent</u> or <u>unpleasant</u>.

Write these ages in the correct order on the lines below.

infant

older adult

newborn

adult

child

toddler

young adult

teenager

Circle the odd word out in each row.

elderly	old-aged	mature	youthful
short	small	beanpole	minuscule
virtuous	spiteful	malevolent	unkind
slender	portly	thin	wiry

Look at the picture of Grandma from *George's Marvellous Medicine*. Fill in her fact file below using as many descriptive words about her as you can. Don't worry if you haven't read the story – use the picture to spark your imagination.

NAME:

APPEARANCE:

PERSONALITY:

BEHAVIOUR:

Beyond the book

Think about the people you see every day. What words would you use to describe them? Remember to be polite!

ANIMALS AND BIRDS

Animals make great story characters, from conniving crocodiles to clever foxes. There are so many different types of animals and birds that we need a lot of words to be able to describe them and the differences between them.

We can put different types of animals into different groups. Read the definitions below. Then draw lines to match each image to its group.

Reptile
Dry scaly skin. Lays eggs on land. Cold-blooded.

Mammal
Warm-blooded. Often covered with hair or fur. Usually gives birth to live young, not eggs.

Invertebrate
No backbone, including insects, worms, spiders and snails.

Bird
Warm-blooded. Lays eggs. Has feathers, wings and a beak.

Amphibian
Cold-blooded. Wet, hairless skin with gills. Lives in water when it's young, then breathes air as an adult.

Fish
Cold-blooded with gills and fins. No arms and legs. Lives in water.

Look at the word web for the Roly-Poly Bird, then use your word knowledge to make a word web for the Enormous Crocodile. You can add more arrows and use the ideas box to help you.

Personality
daring, helpful, compassionate, kind

Sounds
loud voice for singing and calling out a warning

Movements
flies, swoops, swishes and swooshes out of the sky

Appearance
large, colourful, truly magnificent

Body parts
marvellous coloured feathers, beautiful long tail feathers, strong back for carrying monkeys

| greedy | waddle | cunning | swim | leathery |
| sneaky | grin | sharp teeth | scaly | crawl |

PLANTS AND TREES

Have you ever seen a tinkle-tinkle tree or a snozzcumber? Understanding words to describe plants and trees helps you to imagine the scenery in a story, even if they are extra-usual.

Plants include <u>trees</u>, <u>grasses</u>, <u>flowers</u>, <u>herbs</u>, <u>moss</u>, <u>cactuses</u> and <u>weeds</u>. Lots of plants together are called <u>vegetation</u>, and a <u>green</u> landscape could be <u>verdant</u> or <u>lush</u>.

Trees have a <u>trunk</u> covered in <u>bark</u> and its <u>branches</u> could be <u>thick boughs</u> or <u>slender twigs</u>. They might have <u>foliage</u>, <u>blossom</u> or <u>fruit</u>. Trees grow together in a <u>jungle</u> or <u>forest</u>, or can be <u>planted</u> in an <u>orchard</u> or <u>arboretum</u>.

Plants might be <u>leafy</u>, <u>thorny</u>, <u>flowery</u> and <u>fragrant</u>. They might be <u>edible</u> or <u>poisonous</u>.

The root word "arbo" means to do with trees.

arboretum = a place to grow trees

arboriculture = farming or growing of trees

arboreal = living in the treetops

Choose the best word to complete each sentence.

_____ trees keep their leaves all year round.

deciduous / evergreen / flowering

The shrub was extremely _____ to stop animals from eating it.

thorny / lush / edible

The thick green _____ of the trees blocked my view into the forest.

jungle / bark / foliage

The girl climbed the tree's _____ with amazing agility.

stem / trunk / stalk

I am a Geraneous Giraffe and a Geraneous Giraffe cannot eat anything except the pink and purple flowers of the tinkle-tinkle tree.

Because Giraffe can only eat the flowers of the tinkle-tinkle tree, she is delighted to see one. Label the picture of the tinkle-tinkle tree with lots of descriptive words and phrases.

Invent a new type of plant. Draw it below, and then write about it choosing words that help the reader to picture exactly how it looks.

23

MAGICAL CREATURES

Magical creatures can take any form – sometimes literally! You might come across legendary creatures or fantastical new inventions with *frightswiping* powers.

Roald Dahl has written about fantastic creatures such as giants and witches, as well as minpins (tiny people as big as a finger who live high in the trees), whangdoodles, hornswogglers and snozzwangers (terrifying, predatory creatures from Loompaland).

You have probably heard of dragons, unicorns, phoenixes, mermaids and centaurs. But, what about selkies, griffins, nymphs, cockatrices and manticores?

Match the words to their definitions.

noble	a creature that can spit poison a long way
predatory	a creature that eats other animals
manticore	a bird that is reborn after bursting into flames
monstrous	a creature with a scorpion's tail
phoenix	like a scary and unpleasant creature
venomous squerkle	a creature that hunts other creatures
carnivorous	being fine and good

What is the difference between "predatory" and "carnivorous"?

Is it possible for a creature to be "monstrous" and "noble"?

Billy and the Minpins features two fearsome creatures, the Terrible Bloodsuckling Toothpluckling Stonechuckling Spittler and the Red-Hot Smoke-Belching Gruncher!

We can make new adjectives by adding a noun to a verb, like *toothplucking* or *smoke-belching*. Use the words below to make some creatures of your own.

NOUN	VERB	NAME	MY CREATURES:
blood	gobbling	grabber	Slime-Gobbling Grabber
magic	drinking	chuckler	
moon	glugging	tickler	
happiness	throwing	gobbler	
ice	collecting	stomper	
slime	spraying	cruncher	
joy	snatching	yowler	

Beyond the book

Write a story about one of your creatures. What exciting things would happen in it?

FEELINGS AND EMOTIONS

Emotions can drive a story, like the girl's anger in *The Magic Finger*. Understanding just how someone is feeling helps you follow a narrative.

When you are happy, you could be <u>cheerful</u>, <u>delighted</u> or <u>in high spirits</u> – you might <u>grin</u> or <u>chuckle</u>. But sometimes you will be <u>miserable</u>, <u>downcast</u> or <u>disconsolate</u>, and you might <u>sigh</u> or <u>sob</u>. A main character could be <u>plucky</u> or <u>courageous</u>, or be <u>timid</u> and <u>anxious</u>, or find themselves <u>breaking into a cold sweat</u>. When they get <u>angry</u>, they could <u>lose their temper</u> and become <u>furiously irate</u> and <u>see red</u>. Eventually they might <u>regain their composure</u> and become <u>calm</u>.

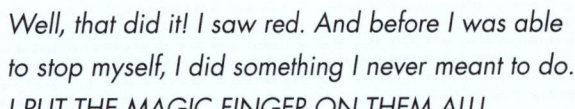

Well, that did it! I saw red. And before I was able to stop myself, I did something I never meant to do. I PUT THE MAGIC FINGER ON THEM ALL!

Circle the two words with the closest meaning in each row.

happy	sigh	nervous	calm	cheerful
troubled	fearless	curious	courageous	in high spirits
anxious	seeing red	furious	disconsolate	grin
contented	enraged	fun	miserable	downcast
composed	scared	jolly	tranquil	chuckle
unsure	plucky	unhappy	elated	timid

Underline the words and phrases in the story text below that show you the girl is losing her temper.

The Magic Finger is something I have been able to do all my life.

I can't tell you just how I do it, because I don't even know myself.

But it always happens when I get cross, when I see red . . .

Then I get very, very hot all over . . .

Then the tip of the forefinger of my right hand begins to tingle most terribly . . .

And suddenly a sort of flash comes out of me, a quick flash, like something electric.

It jumps out and touches the person who has made me cross . . .

What other words and phrases could you use to describe her feelings when the Magic Finger happens?

What words and phrases could you use to describe the girl when she stops feeling angry?

MOVEMENTS AND ACTIONS

Whether a character is *zippfizzing* or dawdling, how they move can tell you a lot about how they're feeling or what they're doing.

If you're excited, you might jump and bounce, but must be careful not to trip. When you're relaxed, you could amble or stroll leisurely, but if you're rushed you might rocket along speedily.

You might be bored and fidgeting, so put on some music and twirl and sashay! Then, when you're tired, you can snooze before springing back into action.

Write a word in each gap to complete these sentences.

She _____ slowly into the room.

He was so excited, he began to _____ up and down.

She was going so fast, she _____ and fell over.

I was tired and decided to _____ .

Animals don't just run and jump, they can:

dig	skip	slink	gallop	bound
fly	slither	burrow	soar	stalk
swim	slide	scuttle	stampede	creep
hop	glide	climb	hover	crawl

Use some of the words above to describe how these animals move.

A fox making a tunnel _____

A wasp at a picnic _____

A snake in the undergrowth _____

A tiger hunting _____

How living things move can tell you a lot about how they feel. Underline the words in the story text below that tell you how Mr Fox is moving.

> Mr Fox crept up the dark tunnel to the mouth of his hole. He poked his long handsome face out into the night air and sniffed once. He moved an inch or two forward and stopped. He sniffed again.

How is Mr Fox feeling in this part of the story?

Underline the words in this story text that tell you how Mr Fox is moving.

> "I've done it!" he yelled. "I've done it first time! I've done it! I've done it!" He pulled himself up through the gap in the floor and started prancing and dancing with joy.

How is Mr Fox feeling now?

Write some words to describe how you would move or what you would do if you felt:

happy	**restless**	**exhausted**

SPEAKING AND VOICES

Is your voice hushy quiet or deep and booming? Everyone has their own way of speaking that makes them unique. Miss Honey and Miss Trunchbull have completely opposite characters, and the way they talk is completely opposite, too!

When you <u>speak loudly</u>, you might <u>proclaim</u>, <u>bellow</u>, <u>roar</u>, <u>thunder</u> or <u>shout</u>. You might speak <u>excitedly</u>, <u>furiously</u>, <u>frantically</u> or even <u>hysterically</u>.

When you <u>speak quietly</u>, you could <u>mumble</u>, <u>murmur</u>, <u>mutter</u> or <u>purr</u>. You might <u>whisper</u> a secret, <u>confiding</u> in someone. You might speak <u>softly</u>, <u>faintly</u> or <u>under your breath</u>.

You might speak <u>clearly</u>, <u>articulately</u> and <u>eloquently</u>, or you may get <u>tongue-tied</u>. You might be <u>chatty</u> and <u>talkative</u>, or you might be <u>reserved</u> and <u>uncommunicative</u>.
As well as speaking, you could <u>sing</u>, <u>chorus</u>, <u>trill</u> or <u>warble</u>.

Underline the words that Roald Dahl uses instead of "said" in this story text from *Matilda* below.

> "How perfectly ridiculous!" snorted the Trunchbull. "[. . .] You're not meant to teach poetry when you're teaching spelling. Cut it out in future, Miss Honey."
>
> "But it does teach them some of the harder words wonderfully well," Miss Honey murmured.
>
> "Don't argue with me, Miss Honey!" the Headmistress thundered.

What does this story text tell you about each character?

Miss Trunchbull is _____

Miss Honey is _____

How many other words can you think of to describe how Miss Trunchbull and Miss Honey speak?

MISS TRUNCHBULL

snorted

thundered

MISS HONEY

murmured

Write a dialogue between two other characters who speak in very different ways. Remember to use lots of varied words to describe how they speak.

THE SENSES

People and animals use their five senses – sight, sound, touch, smell and taste – to experience the world around them. There are lots of words you can use when you talk about the senses.

When you look, you might glimpse or observe something, such as a wonderful vision or a dazzling spectacle. When you hear loud sounds, they might be deafening or thunderous. A nice sound might be melodious. When you touch something, the texture could be smooth, rough, icy or scalding. If you have a good sense of smell, you'll be able to detect pleasant aromas and fragrances, and nasty smells like stenches, pongs and whiffs. The taste of something might be delectable or nauseating.

When you find a sensation indescribable, you might invent your own word to express what you're experiencing. Food could be *uckyslush* or *lickswishy*, or you might put your hand in something *squishous*.

Read the story text below where the BFG describes what sounds he can hear.

"Sometimes, on a very clear night [. . .] I is sometimes hearing faraway music coming from the stars in the sky."

What else might the BFG hear?

the deafening sound of a ladybird walking

Choose some words (or invent some) to describe each of these experiences.

the sound of beautiful singing

the smell of a dustbin

the taste of a delicious cake

the sight of a sunset

the feel of a scratchy jumper

Imagine a new character with a different sense that is as powerful as the BFG's hearing. Use the words on the opposite page and any other words you can think of to write about what they can sense.

PLACES AND SETTINGS

Stories can be set anywhere, from a tiny cottage in the country to a space hotel. Get ready to explore vocabulary that can take you on a wild adventure.

In this section, you'll meet some words about: being at home, exploring cities, life in the country, under the sea, outer space and magical places.

Places from books
Read this description of the Space Hotel from *Charlie and the Great Glass Elevator*.

> . . . the United States of America had successfully launched its first Space Hotel, a gigantic sausage-shaped capsule no less than one thousand feet long. It was called Space Hotel "U.S.A." and it was the marvel of the space age. It had inside it a tennis court, a swimming pool, a gymnasium, a children's playroom and five hundred luxury bedrooms, each with a private bath. It was fully air-conditioned.

Think about a place from a book that you love. It might be a real place or an imaginary one. In the box below, write some words to describe the place.

Draw a picture of this place, using the words you thought of on page 34 to help you add detail.

AT HOME

Human beans need homes, and homes come in many shapes and sizes. There are some *spliffing* words to describe them that also come in many shapes and sizes!

Your home is your residence. You might live in a flat or an apartment or a house. A cottage is a small house, usually in the countryside. A house without an upstairs is a bungalow. Some people even live in castles.

A small home might be cosy and homely, whereas you could describe a large home as palatial and spacious.

Connect each word to its definition.

residence	a very large house
bungalow	big and grand, like a palace
mansion	the place where you live
palatial	a house all on one level
cosy	small and comfortable

Underline the adjectives that describe Miss Honey's cottage in the story text below.

The cottage was so small it looked more like a doll's house than a human dwelling. The bricks it was built of were old and crumbly and very pale red. It had a grey slate roof and one small chimney, and there were two little windows at the front. Each window was no larger than a sheet of tabloid newspaper and there was clearly no upstairs to the place.

Describe the inside of the cottage. Think carefully about the words you use.

Do you think Miss Honey's cottage is a happy place to live? Why or why not?

Now finish this description of an enormous mansion.

Soon the huge house itself came into view, and what a house it was! It was like a palace! It was bigger than a palace!

CITIES AND TOWNS

Some of the stories you will read are set in cities, full of people, buildings, traffic and excitement! Here are some words to describe the bright lights of cities and towns.

Cities and towns are <u>urban</u> places, unlike the countryside which is <u>rural</u>. You will find <u>shopping centres</u>, <u>restaurants</u> and <u>offices</u> in <u>skyscrapers</u>. You might even find that <u>sports stadiums</u>, <u>art galleries</u> and <u>museums</u> have been constructed there. Cities can be <u>modern</u>, full of <u>glass</u> and <u>steel</u>, and can house <u>ancient stone buildings</u>.

Life in the city can be <u>lively</u>, but it can also be <u>noisy</u>. <u>Parks</u> can provide a <u>haven</u> amongst all the <u>hustle and bustle</u>.

Fill the boxes below with new words from this page or words you already know. If you need some inspiration, have a look in some books! Try reading the description of New York in *James and the Giant Peach*.

Positive words and phrases about cities and towns

Negative words and phrases about cities and towns

Circle the closest antonym (word with the opposite meaning) in each group.

peaceful

calm   built-up

bustling   huge

ancient

metropolitan   modern

castle   hectic

clean

crowded   urban

fast-paced   polluted

urban

calm   busy

green   rural

Read the story text below from *The BFG*.

"We is coming close to London," the BFG said.

He slowed to a trot. He began looking about cautiously.

Groups of houses were now appearing on all sides.

Write a description of what Sophie and the BFG could see in a busy city. You can write about London, a city near you or an imaginary city. Use some of the words on page 38 for inspiration.

COUNTRYSIDE AND NATURE

Far from the busy city lies the peace and quiet of the countryside. There are lots of useful words you might come across when your characters are surrounded by *fields and woody hills* like Danny and his father in *Danny the Champion of the World*.

In the countryside, you might find woodland and meadows, as well as rivers and streams. The landscape could be criss-crossed with hedgerows. The lush, green country will be dotted with villages and farms.

You might describe beautiful countryside as being picturesque or scenic. However, it might also be a wild or windswept wilderness.

Choose a word to complete these sentences.

The stream running across the meadow made it a _____ scene.

> picturesque / barren / busy

The wet rock underneath our feet was slippery, so the journey was _____.

> windswept / tranquil / treacherous

The squirrels frolicked high in the trees of the _____.

> hamlet / woodland / meadow

We picked up our backpacks and set off again across the bare, _____ wilderness.

> pretty / dotted / barren

It was a _____ morning and the only sound was birdsong.

> rural / lush / tranquil

40

Read the story text below, from *Danny, the Champion of the World*, and underline your favourite countryside words and phrases.

The world I lived in consisted only of the filling station, the workshop, the wagon, the school, and of course the woods and fields and streams in the countryside around. [. . .]

We sat on the grassy bank below the hedge, waiting for darkness to fall. The sun had set now and the sky was a pale smoke blue, faintly glazed with yellow. In the wood behind us the shadows and the spaces in between the trees were turning from grey to black. [. . .]

And after that we would set off with the sandwiches in our pockets, striding up over Cobblers Hill and down the other side to the small wood of larch trees with the stream running through it.

Now choose four countryside words or phrases from the text, and write definitions for them below.

Word or phrase	Definition
grassy	covered in grass like a green field or meadow

WILD PLACES

Just as there are many wild and wonderful landscapes and climates across the globe, there are a multitude of words to describe these varied vistas: from jungles and forests to mountains, deserts and Giant Country.

Some parts of the <u>natural world</u> might be <u>stunning</u> and <u>majestic</u> but, watch out, because they can also be <u>dangerous</u> or <u>treacherous</u>. <u>Jungles</u> and <u>rainforests</u> are <u>verdant</u> with <u>dense</u>, <u>tangled foliage</u>.

A range of <u>mountains</u> starts in the <u>foothills</u>, climbing up the <u>steep slopes</u> to the <u>summit</u>. Along the way, you might encounter <u>caves</u> and <u>caverns</u> that lead to a <u>subterranean</u> world.

<u>Deserts</u> are <u>desolate</u> places. These <u>wastelands</u> might be <u>sandy</u> or <u>rocky</u>, where only <u>sparse vegetation</u> grows, such as <u>cactuses</u> and <u>snozzcumbers</u>.

Circle the closest synonym (word with a similar meaning) in each group.

barren	**peak**	**rocky**
hot sandy	climb high	mountainous craggy
arid overgrown	snow-capped summit	boulder sandy

knotted	**treetops**	**underground**
jumbled lumpy	leaves canopy	deep cave
tangled tight	undergrowth greenery	subterranean dark

42

Read these sentences from *The BFG* carefully, and use the words to try and visualize each scene. Then draw a picture to match what you imagined.

He went rattling through a great forest, then down into a valley and up over a range of hills as bare as concrete . . .

Soon he was galloping over a desolate wasteland that was not quite of this earth. The ground was flat and pale yellow. Great lumps of blue rock were scattered around, and dead trees stood everywhere like skeletons.

Draw another wild place that the BFG might travel through. Then write a description of it.

SEAS AND OCEANS

The sea is a fascinating place with mysterious depths. It can look different every day depending on the weather. There are many words that can take you away to a beach holiday or thrust you into a watery adventure.

The <u>surface</u> of the sea might be <u>calm</u> and <u>glassy</u>, or it might be <u>foaming</u> and <u>choppy</u>.

In the <u>depths</u>, you might find a <u>coral reef</u> teeming with <u>marine life</u>. The land meets the <u>sea</u> at the <u>shore</u>. A <u>pebbly</u> or <u>sandy shoreline</u> is called a <u>beach</u>. Ships can <u>shelter</u> in a <u>harbour</u>.

Travelling on the seas, you might see <u>yachts</u> or <u>tankers</u>. On the <u>seabed</u>, you might see a <u>shipwreck</u> which has sunk to a <u>watery grave</u>.

Read the story text below from *James and the Giant Peach*.

> *"I told you we were bobbing up and down," the Ladybird said.*
>
> *"We're in the middle of the sea!" cried James.*
>
> *And indeed they were. A strong current and a high wind had carried the peach so quickly away from the shore that already the land was out of sight. All around them lay the vast black ocean, deep and hungry. Little waves were bibbling against the sides of the peach.*

Using the context, what do you think *bibbling* means?

Why do you think Roald Dahl describes the sea as a *vast black ocean, deep and hungry*?

Write what you think will happen next in the story. Use some interesting sea and ocean words!

Match the words to their antonyms.

calm	desolate
surface	fall
rise	sink
teeming	rough
float	seabed

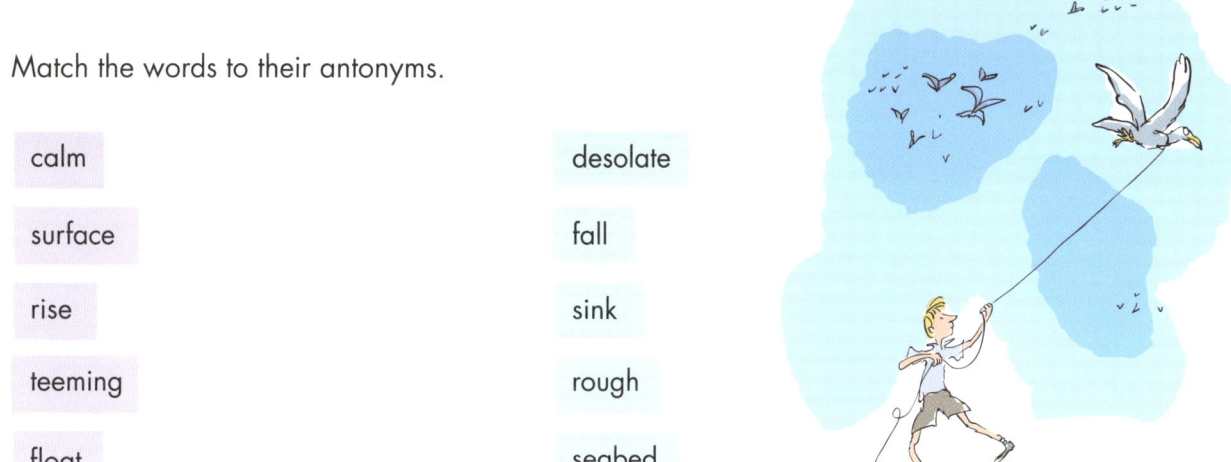

Can you describe each of the things below? You can use new words you've discovered in this book or words you already know.

the rise and fall of the sea

a raging storm

a very calm sea

creatures that live under the sea

BEYOND THE EARTH

Space provides an exciting setting for atmospheric stories. There are many cosmic words that will describe this incredible environment – just watch out for *frightswiping* extra-terrestrials!

First you'll <u>blast off</u> and leave <u>Earth's atmosphere</u> on the way to <u>outer space</u>. You'll need a <u>rocket</u>, <u>spaceship</u> or <u>shuttle</u> to travel in.

<u>Earth</u> is part of the <u>solar system</u>, a group of <u>planets orbiting</u> the <u>Sun</u>, which is a <u>star</u>. Within the <u>boundless expanse</u> of space, you might encounter <u>meteors</u> or <u>shooting stars</u>, or find a way to be transported to other <u>planets</u>. Perhaps you'll see a <u>UFO</u>, an <u>alien</u> or an <u>extra-terrestrial</u>!

In each row, circle the two words with the closest meaning.

| space | luminous | lightspeed | intersteller | bright |

| vast | cold | dark | atmosphere | huge |

| Earth | universe | stratosphere | Sun | cosmos |

| satellite | space shuttle | alien | extra-terrestrial | beyond |

How are interplanetary and interstellar travel different?

Infinite means to go on forever. What do you think finite means?

Can you think of another word that shares a root with infinite?

Read the story text below from *Charlie and the Great Glass Elevator*.

> "These Vermicious Knids are the terror of the Universe. They travel through space in great swarms, landing on other stars and planets and destroying everything they find. There used to be some rather nice creatures living on the moon a long time ago. They were called Poozas. But the Vermicious Knids ate the lot. They did the same on Venus and Mars and many other planets."

Use some astronomically exciting words to describe the Vermicious Knids that are travelling through space.

EXTRAORDINARY PLACES

Extraordinary places don't need to be real: marvellous chocolate factories and jungles full of *whangdoodles* can be conjured up from the imagination. And there are plenty of extraordinary words to tell other people all about them.

Extraordinary places might be legendary. If they are from a time that hasn't happened yet, they are futuristic. A perfect world is a utopia, and a terrible world is a dystopia. An extraordinary place might be natural. Perhaps it is a gloomy cave, lit only by the glistening of shimmering stalactites. It could be built by people or creatures: an enchanted castle or an underwater city, crafted from shells. It could even be a marvellous chocolate factory!

Match the words to their definitions.

obstacles	covered, so you can no longer see it
glistening	not natural – created by humans
shrouded	things that block or get in the way
futuristic	very modern as if set in the future
utopia	very great
tremendous	shining or sparkling with light
artificial	an imagined place where everything is perfect

In each row, circle the two words with the closest meaning.

shrouded	shimmering	dark	glistening	light
obstacles	wonders	sights	marvels	gold
magnificent	awful	champion	tremendous	utopia
found	crafted	built	ship	carried

Read this extract from *Charlie and the Chocolate Factory*.

Mr Wonka opened the door. Five children and nine grown-ups pushed their ways in – and oh, what an amazing sight it was that now met their eyes!

They were looking down upon a lovely valley. There were green meadows on either side of the valley, and along the bottom of it there flowed a great brown river.

What is more, there was a tremendous waterfall halfway along the river – a steep cliff over which the water curled and rolled in a solid sheet, and then went crashing down into a boiling churning whirlpool of froth and spray.

Below the waterfall (and this was the most astonishing sight of all), a whole mass of enormous glass pipes were dangling down into the river from somewhere high up in the ceiling!

It's all chocolate! Every drop of that river is hot melted chocolate of the finest quality!

Circle three extraordinary things in the scene above.

Write a description of two more amazing sights you might see inside the chocolate factory from your own imagination.

OBJECTS AND ITEMS

In this section, you'll explore words for all sorts of amazing things, both from the imagination of Roald Dahl and the real world.

Everyday objects, awesome items, imaginary stuff and the equally important words we need to describe them – they're all here. You'll meet words for food, transport, inventions, machines, and magical potions and spells.

Look around the room you're in. Write down the most interesting object and the most boring object you can see. Think of some words to describe them. Make them sound as interesting and boring as you possibly can.

Most interesting

Most boring

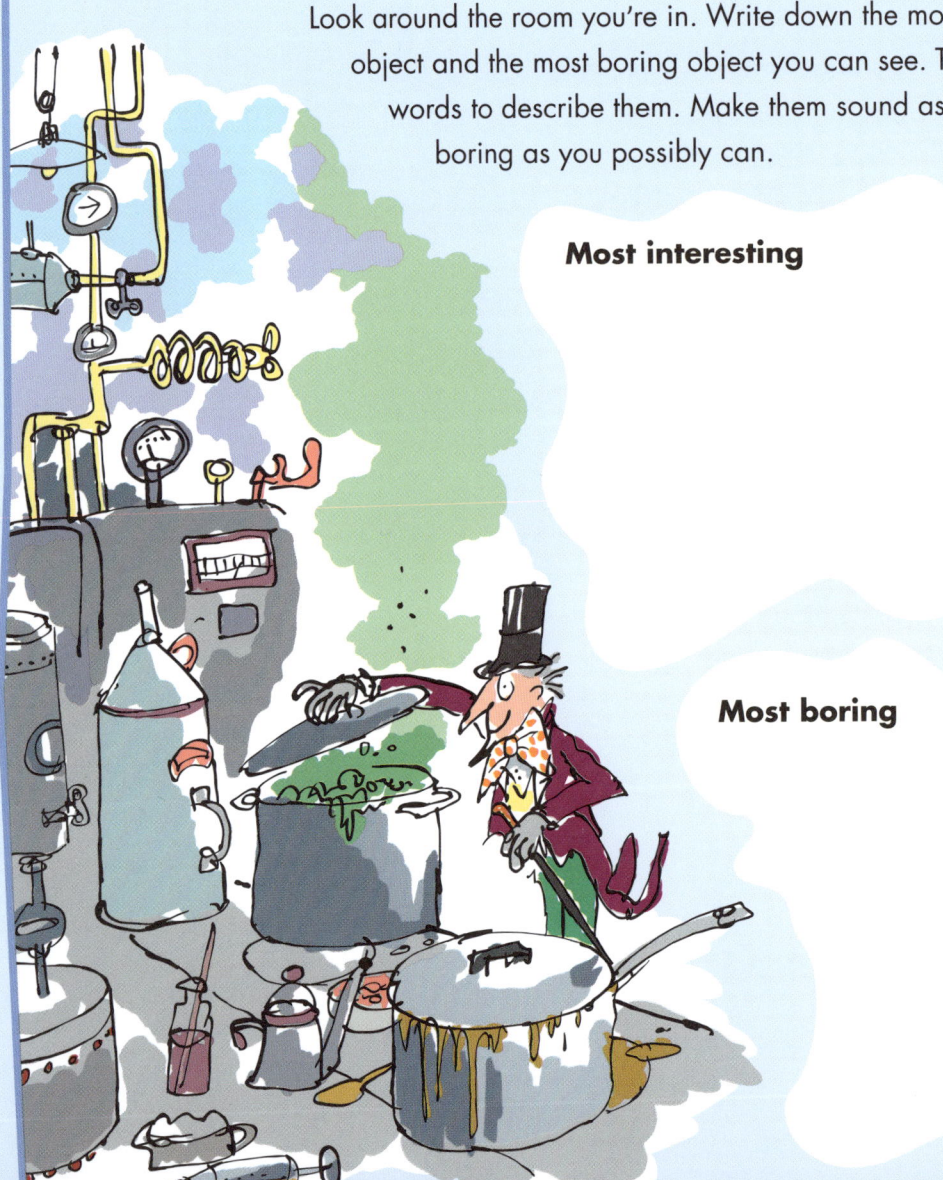

Read this description of one of the machines in the chocolate factory.

> *It was a mountain of gleaming metal that towered high above the children and their parents. Out of the very top of it there sprouted hundreds and hundreds of thin glass tubes.*

Words for inventions

Willy Wonka has thought of a new invention. It might be a delicious new sweet, a clever machine or a brilliant way to travel. Draw his latest invention and label it.

FOOD

Whether your dinner is *lickswishy* and *delumptious* or *rotsome* and *disgustive*, it can be lots of fun finding words to describe flavour.

You might enjoy a meal, grab a quick snack or settle down for a feast or banquet. If you're hungry, famished or ravenous (or just greedy and gluttonous), you might gobble your food or gorge on it. If you have a smaller appetite, you might pick at or nibble a snack.

Food might be sweet or savoury. It could be chewy and leathery, or crisp and crunchy.

Delicious food might be appetizing, ambrosial, delectable or scrumdiddlyumptious. Disgusting food could be unpalatable, disagreeable, indigestible or nauseating enough to make you feel sick. Or it could be as tasteless and bland as cardboard!

When you are cooking, you might bake, roast, boil, fry, grill, poach or stew your ingredients before serving them up. A dish can be the crockery you serve the food on or the food itself.

Choose the best word to complete each of these sentences.

After the _____, I was so full I couldn't move!

| appetite / snack / banquet |

He was _____, so he ate the whole chocolate bar in one gulp.

| ambrosial / famished / mushy |

The snozzcumber tasted _____, so he spat it out at once.

| disgusting / savoury / ravenous |

The bread was as _____ as old leather, but he tried to finish it.

| chewy / bland / delectable |

Write some words or phrases to describe the scrumptious or *repulsant* foods in each of the boxes.

chocolate cake

a fresh snozzcumber

bird pie

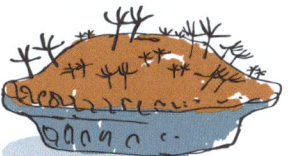

Draw the most delicious and the most disgusting foods you can imagine, then describe them.

The most delicious foods

The most disgusting foods

Beyond the book

Next time you're eating something particularly delicious or disgusting, think of the best words to describe it. If it's not very nice, remember not to share those words with the cook!

TRANSPORT

Whether you trundle along by tractor or go *zipfizzing* off in a rocket, there are lots of interesting words to describe any kind of journey you can imagine.

You might travel on the road in a car or on a bus or motorcycle. On the water, you could be on a ferry or cruise ship, or paddling in a kayak. An aeroplane, helicopter or hot air balloon could carry you in the air. You can travel on tracks on a train or steam engine, or under your own steam on a bicycle or by foot.

A rough journey might be jarring or jolting. A smooth trip would be calm and level. However you travel, hopefully your voyage will be plain sailing.

Write a word or phrase to describe each of the following.

a canoe on a calm lake

a bicycle on bumpy mud track

a high-speed train

Look at the words below. What kinds of transport do you think they describe, and where are they going?

jolting

rapid

plain sailing

Read the story text below from *James and the Giant Peach*.

In the whole history of the world, no travellers had ever had a more terrible journey than these unfortunate creatures. It had started out well, with much laughing and shouting, and for the first few seconds, as the peach had begun to roll slowly forward, nobody had minded being tumbled about a little bit. And when it went BUMP! and the Centipede had shouted, "That was Aunt Sponge!" and then BUMP! again, and "That was Aunt Spiker!" there had been a tremendous burst of cheering all around.

But as soon as the peach rolled out of the garden and began to go down the steep hill, rushing and plunging and bounding madly downward, then the whole thing became a nightmare.

In the story text above, circle four verbs that describe the way the giant peach travels.

Would you describe James's journey as "jarring and jerky" or "smooth and easy-going"? Why?

Write a short description of the giant peach travelling smoothly through the air.

INVENTORS AND INVENTIONS

An inventor is a person who designs and creates marvellous and *wondercrump* inventions. Get the cogs in your brainbox whirring by learning some *splendiferous* words that describe ingenious inventions.

An <u>innovation</u> might <u>solve a problem</u> or come about because the <u>inventor</u> has had a <u>flash of inspiration</u>.

<u>Inventors</u> are often <u>imaginative</u>, <u>intelligent</u> people who <u>create</u> <u>ingenious</u> new <u>machines</u>, <u>gadgets</u>, <u>contraptions</u> or <u>gizmos</u>. They could <u>build</u>, <u>manufacture</u> or <u>assemble</u> these themselves, or they might work with others to <u>construct</u> them.

<u>Genius inventors</u> don't just make machines, they might invent new foods, too . . .

Read the story text below about inventor Willy Wonka.

> *"He has some really fantastic inventions up his sleeve, Mr Willy Wonka has! Did you know that he's invented a way of making chocolate ice cream so that it stays cold for hours and hours without being in the refrigerator? You can even leave it lying in the sun all morning on a hot day and it won't go runny!"*

Underline the words that tell you that Willy Wonka is a clever inventor.

Write a description of a terrible inventor. What is their name? Why do their ideas go wrong?

_____
_____
_____
_____

Pick some punchy vocabulary to complete this job advertisement.

WANTED: INVENTOR

We are looking for a _____ and _____

inventor for our factory! A sense of _____ will help you to make new

_____.

Personality: You must be _____ and _____.

Skills: You must be able to _____ machines and other

_____.

Draw a new mechanical invention, and write a description of what your machine does. Let your imagination run wild – your gadget can do anything!

POTIONS AND SPELLS

The world of magic provides a rich source of spellbinding new words: words for magic, words for spells and words for the things that magic can do!

People with <u>magical powers</u> such as <u>witches</u>, <u>magicians</u>, <u>sorcerers</u> and <u>enchanters</u> can <u>cast spells</u> which might <u>bewitch</u> people.

As well as <u>casting charms</u> and <u>curses</u>, they can <u>mix potions</u> which might begin to <u>bubble</u>, <u>froth</u>, <u>fizz</u> or <u>gurgle</u>. These may give off <u>colourful smoke</u> or <u>noxious fumes</u>. The witch or wizard may need to <u>chant</u> an <u>incantation</u> while they <u>stir</u> the <u>mixture</u>.

Magic potions and spells might be concocted by a witch, like The Grand High Witch's Formula 86 Delayed Action Mouse-Maker in *The Witches*.

> "Next," said The Grand High Witch, "you take your boiled telescope and your frrried mouse tails and your cooked mice and your rrroasted alarm clock and all together you put them into the mixer. Then you mix them at full speed. This vill give you a nice thick paste. Vhile the mixer is still mixing you must add to it the yolk of vun grrruntle's egg."

Copy three verbs from the story text that tell the other witches what to do with their ingredients.

Match the ingredients to the effect they might have on the drinker of the potion.

boiled wrong end of a telescope	will turn children into mice
roasted alarm-clock	will shrink children
cooked mice and fried mouse-tails	will cause the transformation to be delayed and happen later

It isn't just witches and wizards that can make magical potions. Read the story text below from *George's Marvellous Medicine* about George making his medicine, and underline your three favourite words or phrases.

Soon the marvellous mixture began to froth and foam. A rich blue smoke, the colour of peacocks, rose from the surface of the liquid, and a fiery fearsome smell filled the kitchen. It made George choke and splutter. It was a smell unlike any he had smelled before. It was a brutal and bewitching smell, spicy and staggering, fierce and frenzied, full of wizardry and magic. Whenever he got a whiff of it up his nose, firecrackers went off in his skull and electric prickles ran along the backs of his legs. It was wonderful to stand there stirring this amazing mixture and to watch it smoking blue and bubbling and frothing and foaming as though it were alive.

Write a word from the story text to match each definition.

| **lots of small bubbles which form in a liquid** | **strong and powerful** |

| **enchanting and magical** | **moving from the bottom to the top** |

George is about to add something else to the pan. Use words from this page (or that you know already) to write a description of what he adds and what happens to the medicine.

59

LITTLE WORDS, BIG DIFFERENCE

One tiny little word can change the whole meaning of a sentence. In this section, you'll look at the smallest, but most important, words.

The BFG is full of amazing words you don't hear every day, and a lot of them are completely made up. When you are reading, it is tempting to concentrate on the meaning of the interesting, unfamiliar and sometimes invented words.

HUMPLECRIMP

BIFFSQUIGGLE

TROGGLEHUMPER

CRODSCOLLOP

But actually, it's often the small, everyday words that help us understand the meaning of other words and build a picture of the text.

THE   THAT   BUT   WILL

AND   SO   WOULD SO

A   THIS

Think of the little, common words that you use most often, and write them below.

You might have learned about determiners, modal verbs and conjunctions already. If so, fill out the table below with all the words you know in each category.

Don't worry if this is all new – just carry straight on through the book and come back to this page once you've learned all about these useful words!

Determiners

| an | these | some |

Modal verbs

| could | might | should |

Conjunctions

| and | because | so |

DETERMINERS

Determiners are words that introduce a noun. They can give you lots of useful information and help you to picture the scene precisely.

Determiners can tell you which noun is being talked about, where it is, whose it is and how many of it there are.

The **indefinite article** refers to any noun:
<u>A</u> tin of Hugtight Sticky Glue

The **definite article** refers to a particular noun: <u>The</u> tin of Hugtight Sticky Glue

Demonstrative determiners show position:

<u>That</u> wormy spaghetti

<u>This</u> normal spaghetti

Possessive determiners show ownership:

<u>Your</u> glass eye

<u>My</u> glass eye

Quantifiers tell you the number or amount:

<u>Many</u> birds

<u>Four</u> birds

Choose a determiner to complete these sentences from *The Twits* below.

Mr Twit was one of _____ very hairy-faced men.

that / these / any / his

Muggle-Wump and his family longed to escape from _____ cage in Mr Twit's garden.

five / some / the / few

If you have good thoughts, they will shine out of _____ face like sunbeams.

an / less / your / nine

Sort these determiners into the boxes below.

| the | this | those | less | a | any | your | nine |
| her | more | his | our | these | few | many | |

Definite and indefinite articles

an

Demonstrative determiners

that

Possessive determiners

my

Quantifiers

five
some

Underline the determiners below.

Then all at once she felt something cold and slimy crawling over her feet. She screamed.

"What's the matter with you?" Mr Twit said.

"Help!" screamed Mrs Twit, bouncing about. "There's something in my bed!"

"I'll bet it's that Giant Skillywiggler I saw on the floor just now," Mr Twit said.

How do the determiners <u>my</u> bed and <u>that</u> Giant Skillywiggler help to explain why Mrs Twit is very scared?

63

MODAL VERBS

Modal verbs change the meaning of other verbs. The most common modal verbs are will, would, can, could, may, might, shall, should, must and ought.

Read the extracts below from *Charlie and the Great Glass Elevator*, and use the modal verbs to help you answer the questions.

> "You mean . . . there <u>might</u> be swarms of [Gnoolies] all around us this very moment?" Charlie asked.
>
> "There <u>might</u>," said Mr Wonka.

Are there definitely swarms of Gnoolies surrounding the Great Glass Elevator? How do you know?

_____

_____

> "WE <u>SHALL</u> THEN PRESS THE EMERGENCY FREEZER SWITCH AND THE TEMPERATURE IN THE SPACE HOTEL <u>WILL</u> DROP TO MINUS ONE HUNDRED DEGREES CENTIGRADE. ALL OF YOU <u>WILL</u> BE INSTANTLY DEEP FROZEN."

Would this speech seem as threatening if it said, "We <u>might</u> press the freezer switch"?

_____

_____

> "Wait a minute! You look younger than thirty! You can't be a day more than twenty now! . . . But that's enough, isn't it! . . . I should stop there if I were you! Twenty's quite young enough! . . ."

Which modal verb in Grandpa Joe's speech tells you that he wants Grandma Josephine to stop growing younger?

_____

Write some advice for each of the situations below, using one of the modal verbs in the box. The first one has been done for you as an example.

The Great Glass Elevator shot into the air.

should / will / may

Everyone should hold on tight!

The Space Hotel "U.S.A." was a wonderful place, orbiting the Earth.

must / might / would

Huge, angry Vermicious Knids have been spotted in the area.

will / shouldn't / can

WONKA-VITE is a new vitamin invented by Willy Wonka. Each pill will make you YOUNGER by exactly 20 years.

could / must / ought to

CONJUNCTIONS

Conjunctions are words that are used to link two parts of a sentence together. When you are reading, conjunctions can reveal the meaning of a sentence like magic, by explaining the relationship between different ideas in it.

Conjunctions might be used to express time:

> In every case a strange lady was seen outside the house, <u>just</u> before it happened.

Or they might tell you that one thing causes another:

> I cannot explain how it worked <u>because</u> I know nothing about electricity.

Choose a conjunction to complete these sentences from *The Witches*:

There was a door connecting my room with my grandmother's room _____ that we could visit each other without going into the corridor.

because / so / before

I myself had two separate encounters with witches _____ I was eight years old.

or / and / before

Look carefully at the eyes, _____ the eyes of a real witch are different from yours and mine.

because / yet / so

Use a conjunction to join these pairs of sentences together to make one sentence.

A witch's eye will keep changing colour. You will see fire and ice there.

_____

_____

_____

Witches have square feet. It makes shoes uncomfortable.

_____

_____

_____

Witches use their spit as ink. It is blue.

_____

_____

_____

A witch might hold her nose when she meets you. You smell awful to her.

_____

_____

_____

UNDERSTANDING PHRASES

Sometimes phrases have meanings that you can't work out from their individual words. You just have to take a leaf out of Matilda's book and learn them! These are called idioms.

Have you ever heard of someone "pulling someone's leg" or feeling "under the weather"? The idiom "pulling someone's leg" means to joke or tease someone. Feeling "under the weather" means feeling a bit unwell.

Look at the two idioms from *Matilda* underlined below. What do they mean?

> Matilda said, "Never do anything by halves if you want to get away with it. Be outrageous. <u>Go the whole hog</u>. Make sure everything you do is completely unbelievable. No parent is going to believe this pigtail story, <u>not in a million years</u>. Mine wouldn't. They'd call me a liar."

Go the whole hog means

_____

_____

_____

Not in a million years means

_____

_____

_____

Match each idiom to its meaning.

pull someone's leg	to give away a secret
bite the bullet	to avoid saying what you really mean
spill the beans	to do something you have been avoiding
take it with a pinch of salt	to not believe something or not take it seriously
call it a day	to joke or tease someone
feel under the weather	to feel ill
beat around the bush	to stop doing something

Finish each sentence using one of the idioms above that matches with the picture.

After eating a whole cake, Bruce Bogtrotter was feeling _____ .

"Get to the point! Don't _____ ," said Miss Trunchbull.

"You have to _____ , and talk to Miss Trunchbull," said Matilda.

Beyond the book

Do you have a favourite idiom? It could be from any language or culture. Write it below.

_____

MAKING SENSE OF WORDS

Wow, what a lot of words you've learned! Matilda would be proud of you. Now you have a brain bulging with new vocabulary, it's time to look at different ways to read.

In this section, you'll learn some handy strategies to make reading easier and quicker, including: making predictions, drawing inferences, skimming, summarizing and visualizing.

My reading shelf

Write the names of your favourite books in the bookcase below. Next time you read a new book, add it on to your reading shelf.

MAKING PREDICTIONS

Predictions are when you make a sensible guess about what might happen in a story based on what you know already. Developing good prediction skills can also help you spot when something doesn't seem right in a text, and you can read it again more carefully.

Read these sentences from *The Giraffe and the Pelly and Me*, then circle a sensible prediction for what might happen next.

I climbed into the big orange beak, and with a swoosh of wings the Pelican . . .

. . . drove around on a tiny set of wheels.

. . . carried me back to his perch on the windowsill.

. . . swallowed me whole, including my hat.

At exactly that moment, a huge white Rolls-Royce pulled up right below us, and a chauffeur in a blue and gold uniform got out. He . . .

. . . was carrying an envelope in one gloved hand.

. . . started breakdancing on the pavement.

. . . transformed into a large green cat.

The next moment, the Giraffe's neck, which heaven knows was long enough already, began to . . .

. . . shrink until it was very tiny.

. . . grow longer and LONGER and LONGER and LONGER.

. . . flash different colours like a traffic light.

Read the story text below.

> Then the Giraffe, with the Monkey on her head, tiptoed very gingerly away from the house and came towards us. The Pelican flew with them. The Giraffe came up very close to the Duke and whispered, "Your Grace, there is a man in one of the bedrooms on the third floor. He is opening all the drawers and taking things out. He's got a pistol!"

What do you think will happen next?

What do you think is very unlikely to happen next?

MAKING INFERENCES

Sometimes you have to read between the lines to work out information about characters or situations in books. This involves thinking about what the author is suggesting alongside what they have actually written – this is called inference.

Read this description of Miss Trunchbull walking from *Matilda*.

> When she marched – Miss Trunchbull never walked, she always marched like a storm trooper with long strides and arms a-swinging – when she marched along a corridor you could actually hear her snorting as she went, and if a group of children happened to be in her path, she ploughed right on through them like a tank, with small people bouncing off her to left and right.

What can you learn about Miss Trunchbull from the story text?

_____

_____

_____

_____

Now read the four different descriptions. Can you guess how the characters are feeling?

> Miss Honey's mouth dropped open and her eyes stretched so wide you could see the whites all round.

Miss Honey is feeling _____

_____ .

Matilda leapt into Miss Honey's arms and hugged her.

Matilda is feeling _____

_____.

Two red spots appeared on the father's cheeks. "Who the heck do you think you are?" he shouted.

Mr Wormwood is feeling _____

_____.

She glared at Bruce Bogtrotter, who was sitting on his chair like some overstuffed grub, replete, comatose, unable to move or to speak. A fine sweat was beading his forehead but there was a grin of triumph on his face.

Bruce Bogtrotter is feeling _____

_____.

Use the box below to write down the words from the passages above that helped you to answer the questions about making inferences.

VISUALIZE IT

For you to understand exactly what is happening in a scene, sometimes you need to read carefully and slowly, thinking about everything the author describes. As you read, try to create a picture in your head. This is called visualizing.

Read this scene from *Fantastic Mr Fox* carefully and slowly.

> They were still singing as they rounded the final corner and burst in upon the most wonderful and amazing sight any of them had ever seen. The feast was just beginning. A large dining room had been hollowed out of the earth, and in the middle of it, seated around a huge table, were no less than twenty-nine animals. They were:
>
> Mrs Fox and three Small Foxes.
>
> Mrs Badger and three Small Badgers.
>
> Mole and Mrs Mole and four Small Moles.
>
> Rabbit and Mrs Rabbit and five Small Rabbits.
>
> Weasel and Mrs Weasel and six Small Weasels.
>
> The table was covered with chickens and ducks and geese and hams and bacon, and everyone was tucking into the lovely food.
>
> "My darling!" cried Mrs Fox, jumping up and hugging Mr Fox. "We couldn't wait!"

Now read it a second time. As you read, visualize the scene and try to picture:

- what the room looks like
- where the animals are sitting
- what the animals look like
- what is on the table.

> If you aren't able to visualize, don't worry – try a technique on another page.

Now draw a picture of the scene including as much detail as you can.

SKIMMING AND SCANNING

Sometimes we need to read carefully so we know exactly what is happening. But sometimes we can read quickly to get the main idea or find a particular piece of information in a piece of text. These quicker types of reading are called **skimming** and **scanning**.

Skimming is when you read quickly to get a general idea of the text. Skim read the list below from *George's Marvellous Medicine* as quickly as you can.

- GOLDENGLOSS HAIR SHAMPOO
- TOOTHPASTE
- SUPERFOAM SHAVING SOAP
- VITAMIN-ENRICHED FACE CREAM
- NAIL VARNISH
- HAIR REMOVER. SMEAR IT ON YOUR LEGS AND ALLOW TO REMAIN FOR FIVE MINUTES.
- DISHWORTH'S FAMOUS DANDRUFF CURE
- BRILLIDENT FOR CLEANING FALSE TEETH
- NEVERMORE PONKING DEODORANT SPRAY. GUARANTEED TO KEEP AWAY UNPLEASANT BODY SMELLS FOR A WHOLE DAY
- LIQUID PARAFFIN
- HELGA'S HAIRSET. HOLD TWELVE INCHES AWAY FROM THE HAIR AND SPRAY LIGHTLY.
- FLOWERS OF TURNIPS PERFUME
- PINK PLASTER POWDER

What is this a list of?

Which room might George have got these things from?

Scanning is when you read quickly to find a particular word or fact. Scan the list of ingredients on the opposite page to find the answer to these questions.

What is the perfume called?

How long should you leave the hair remover on for?

How should you spray hair with Helga's Hairset?

What is the name of a treatment for dandruff?

Beyond the book

Skimming and scanning are useful skills, but be careful not to use them too often as you might miss important information. When you read, think about when it would be useful to skim or scan, and when you need to read slowly and carefully.

CLARIFYING AND SUMMARIZING

Making sure you have understood the information in the text is important when you are reading. You can do this through clarifying and summarizing.

If you find something you've read confusing, you can pause while you try to work out the meaning of the word or sentence you are stuck on. This is called clarifying. Summarizing is when you recall the main points or ideas once you have finished reading.

There are many strategies you can use to clarify the meaning of the words you read. Put a tick next to the strategies that you like to use.

- [ ] Use the context to work out the meaning of a word.
- [ ] Look to see if you know any other words related to this word.
- [ ] Use prefixes and suffixes to work out the meaning of a word.
- [ ] Look for key words like determiners, modal verbs and conjunctions.
- [ ] Reread the sentence again.
- [ ] Try to visualize what is happening in the text.
- [ ] Make a prediction about what might happen next.
- [ ] Use your background knowledge to make sense of a text.
- [ ] Use clues from the context and pictures.
- [ ] Use the glossary or a dictionary to look up the meaning of a word.

Write a summary of *The Enormous Crocodile*. If you don't know the story, choose another one you know well and summarize it. Design a front cover that goes with your summary.

Beyond the book

Think of another story. It could be from a book, a TV programme or film, or a game you have played. Write a summary of its plot.

PUTTING IT INTO PRACTICE

You've made it! You've learned bucket loads of new words, picked up some strategies for reading confidently and had fun along the way.

Now it's time for you to try out your new vocabulary superpowers.

In this section, you'll find four reading challenges based on *swashboggling* scenes from Roald Dahl's stories. Once you've completed each challenge, you can look up your answers online.

GOOD LUCK!

Challenge leaderboard

Every time you complete a challenge, colour in a prize below.

Danny's challenge

James's challenge

The BFG's challenge

Matilda's challenge

DANNY'S CHALLENGE

Read the section of the story below, then complete the activities. Use all your new reading skills to help you.

In this scene from *Danny the Champion of the World*, Danny is describing his father and his father's smile.

> My father, without the slightest doubt, was the most marvellous and exciting father any child ever had. [. . .]
>
> You might think, if you didn't know him well, that he was a stern and serious man. He wasn't. He was actually a wildly funny person. What made him appear so serious was the fact that he never smiled with his mouth. He did it all with his eyes. He had brilliant blue eyes and when he thought of something funny, his eyes would flash and if you looked carefully, you could actually see a tiny little golden spark dancing in the middle of each eye. But the mouth never moved.
>
> I was glad my father was an eye-smiler. It meant he never gave me a fake smile, because it's impossible to make your eyes twinkle if you aren't feeling twinkly yourself. A mouth-smile is different. You can fake a mouth-smile any time you want, simply by moving your lips. I've also learned that a real mouth-smile always has an eye-smile to go with it, so watch out, I say, when someone smiles at you with their mouth but the eyes stay the same. It's sure to be bogus.
>
> My father was not what you would call an educated man and I doubt if he had read twenty books in his life. But he was a marvellous storyteller. He used to make up a bedtime story for me every single night, and the best ones were turned into serials and went on for many nights running.

1 Find three adjectives that Danny uses to describe his father. Write them below.

2 Match the words to their meanings.

- stern
- twinkle
- bogus
- impossible

- fake or not true
- serious or strict
- sparkle or shine
- can't be done

3 Which phrase tells you that Danny was proud of his father? Write it below.

_____

_____

4 Which does Danny think are better: eye-smiles or mouth-smiles? Why?

_____

_____

5 Write a description of Danny's father as if you were telling someone else about him.

_____

_____

_____

_____

_____

JAMES'S CHALLENGE

Read the section of the story below, then do the activities. Off you go!

In this story text from *James and the Giant Peach*, the peach is floating through the sky, being pulled by hundreds of seagulls.

> James Henry Trotter and his companions crouched close together on top of the peach as the night began closing in around them. Clouds like mountains towered high above their heads on all sides, mysterious, menacing, overwhelming. Gradually it grew darker and darker, and then a pale three-quarter moon came up over the tops of the clouds and cast an eerie light over the whole scene. The giant peach swayed gently from side to side as it floated along, and the hundreds of silky white strings going upward from its stem were beautiful in the moonlight. So also was the great flock of seagulls overhead.
>
> There was not a sound anywhere. Travelling upon the peach was not in the least like travelling in an aeroplane. The aeroplane comes clattering and roaring through the sky, and whatever might be lurking secretly up there in the great cloud-mountains goes running for cover at its approach. That is why people who travel in aeroplanes never see anything.
>
> But the peach . . . ah, yes . . . the peach was a soft, stealthy traveller, making no noise at all as it floated along. And several times during that long silent night ride high up over the middle of the ocean in the moonlight, James and his friends saw things that no one had ever seen before.

1 Find two verbs that describe how the peach moves, and write them below.

2 How might the way the peach moves help James to see *things that no one had ever seen before*? You could use words and phrases from the story in your answer.

3 Match each of these words to its meaning.

companions	hidden, perhaps ready to jump out
eerie	friends or people you travel with
lurking	sneaky or moving carefully so as not to be seen
stealthy	strange or frightening

4 Try to visualize the scene from the peach. Retell it in your own words as if you were James telling someone else about the amazing sights he has seen.

_____

_____

_____

_____

_____

_____

_____

_____

5 Make a prediction about what James might see next.

_____

_____

_____

_____

THE BFG'S CHALLENGE

Read the section of the story below, then complete the activities.
Remember to look at the context!

In this story text from *The BFG*, the Big Friendly Giant, with Sophie hidden in his pocket, has been cornered by the other giants.

> "Here comes the runty one!" boomed the Fleshlumpeater. "Ho-ho there, runty one! Where is you splatch-winkling away to in such a hefty hurry?" He shot out an enormous arm and grabbed the BFG by the hair. The BFG didn't struggle. He simply stopped and stood quite still and said, "Be so kind as to be letting go of my hair, Fleshlumpeater."
>
> The Fleshlumpeater released him and stepped back a pace. The other giants stood around, waiting for the fun to start.
>
> "Now then, you little grobsquiffler!" boomed the Fleshlumpeater. "We is all of us wanting to know where you is galloping off to every day in the daytime. Nobody ought to be galloping off to anywhere until it is getting dark. The human beans could easily be spotting you and starting a giant hunt and we is not wanting that to happen, is we not?"
>
> "We is not!" shouted the other giants. "Go back to your cave, runty one!"
>
> "I is not galloping to any human bean country," the BFG said. "I is going to other places."
>
> "I is thinking," said the Fleshlumpeater, "that you is catching human beans and keeping them as pets!"
>
> "Right you is!" cried the Bloodbottler. "Just now I is hearing him chittering away to one of them in his cave!"

1 Scan the scene above, then use the context to work out what the words below might mean.

splatch-winkling _____

grobsquiffler _____

chittering _____

2 What do you think the giants are planning for the BFG when they say they are *waiting for the fun to start*?

_____

_____

3 Will the giants' plan be fun for the BFG? How do you know?

_____

_____

4 Match each of these words to its meaning.

runty	running quickly and possibly out of control
galloping	small
hefty	forming a tight group around something
clustering	large and heavy

5 Why do you think the BFG did not struggle when the Fleshlumpeater grabbed him by his hair?

_____

_____

MATILDA'S CHALLENGE

Read the section of the story below and then do the activities. Good luck!

In this story text from *Matilda*, Roald Dahl introduces Matilda and her amazing brain.

*It is bad enough when parents treat **ordinary** children as though they were scabs and bunions, but it becomes somehow a lot worse when the child in question is **extra**ordinary, and by that I mean sensitive and brilliant. Matilda was both of these things, but above all she was brilliant. Her mind was so nimble and she was so quick to learn that her ability should have been obvious even to the most half-witted of parents. But Mr and Mrs Wormwood were both so gormless and so wrapped up in their own silly little lives that they failed to notice anything unusual about their daughter. To tell the truth, I doubt they would have noticed had she crawled into the house with a broken leg.*

*Matilda's brother Michael was a perfectly normal boy, but the sister, as I said, was something to make your eyes pop. By the age of **one and a half** her speech was perfect and she knew as many words as most grown-ups. The parents, instead of applauding her, called her a noisy chatterbox and told her sharply that small girls should be seen and not heard.*

*By the time she was **three**, Matilda had taught herself to read by studying newspapers and magazines that lay around the house. At the age of **four**, she could read fast and well and she naturally began hankering after books.*

1 Find two adjectives from above that describe Matilda's mind. Write them below.

2 Match each of these words to its meaning.

nimble	directly and a little angrily
sharply	talent or skill
gormless	quick and agile
ability	foolish or lacking sense

3 Skim the story text to find the numbers written in **bold**. Why do you think these words are emphasized?

_____

_____

4 How are Michael and Matilda different? You can use words from the story in your answer.

_____

_____

_____

5 Describe how Matilda's parents feel about her. Use your own words.

_____

_____

_____

MY SPLENDIFEROUS DICTIONARY

Well done! You are going to be *the most amazing, the most fantastic, the most extraordinary* reader. Whenever you come across a word you want to remember, write it in this dictionary along with its definition. Then you'll know exactly where to find it when you need it.

A

B

C

D

E

F

G

H

I

J

K

L

M

N

O

P

Q

R

S

T

U

V

W

X

Y

Z